What Should Danny Do?

Anger Control Activities for Kids and Teens

Calming Anger Management Workbook Using social skills

NEW - UPDATED VERSION
By

Samantha Williams

TABLE OF CONTENT

A LITTLE STORY 3

EDWARD'S STORY 4

PARENTS HELPING CHILDREN CALM DOWN
NOTES 17

CALMING ANGER WITH THE FOLLOWING
ACTIVITIES 24

ANGER TRIGGERS 28

ANGER THERMOMETER............................33

ANGER COLORING
ACTIVITIES...............................…......................
41

A LITTLE STORY

Welcome. We shall discuss and read about anger control activities. I am sure you are willing to try them out. But first, let's share a story

Edward's Story

Edward was loved by his mum and Dad as a little boy. One day, Edward went outside to play with his friends.

Edward wanted to play, but he wasn't sure WHAT

Game to PLAY?

Should I go to SKATING or SWIMMING?

Edward was watching as other kids Swung around the play Ground

He wished he could have fun with others.

He was watching other kids play must be fun, he said to himself.

yeah! Yeah!

Sooner, his friend calls

Look here, Edward!

Over here, Come Along, let's Play.

Alright. Edward Answered.

He moved toward them and Joined in the Game.

Come over here and have some fun. The kids echoed.

joined **Edward henry to basketball.**

Edward was a very good basketball player. At some point, Henry felt Edward was holding the ball to himself.

You slowpoke. Henry began pulling Edward's shirt. Coward!

Henry yelled.

Edward was surprised! He wanted to reply but wasn't sure of what to say.

Then he left the field in anger.

He went and sat under a tree.

What would he do now?

Should he hit his friend, of course, he was mad at the hurting words henry used today?

He went and sat under an oak tree

While under the tree, he remembered the candy he received from his mother, which he had some left in his pocket.

He brought out some of it and began

 chewing it.

Suddenly, a bully came around and collected the candy from him,

Give me all of it. The bully shouted.

Edward immediately released all the candy in his pocket.

Oh my God, This must have been traumatic for him.

Now he has nothing left to eat. When he got up to leave, one of the kids threw a Paper plane at him.

I've had enough. He said.

I'm going home now. He said.

When he got back, he wasn't happy.

What's wrong? He thought.

I don't know. I feel mad at my friends each time they get on my nerves.

Then, his mother came in; she asked what the problem was.

She then proceeded to make his favorite dish.

Wow! So yummy and sweet. Thanks, mum.

I'm happy you liked it. Now tell me what happened, she queried.

What's the matter, mummy asked? Tell me your experience today; Mummy insisted.

My friends made me **Angry**, and I'm **mad** at them.

Really? Mummy added. Tell me more

They yelled at me during games just because I play better.

They called me **funny names**. And threw things at me.

One of them collected my **candy**.

I feel like hitting each of them.

I'm so sorry, dear. Mummy added. What do I do now? Edward asked

Just a moment!
What would he do?
HELPING CHILDREN CALM DOWN
NOTES FOR PARENTS

Parents can begin by helping kids understand how their feelings work. Children don't go from calm to sobbing on the floor in an instant. They'll build it over time, just like a wave. Kids can learn control by noticing and labeling their feelings earlier before it gets more significant than what they can handle.

Some kids are unwilling to accept negative emotions. When most kids growing up thinks that anxiety, anger, sadness are bad emotions. It's better to name them on time, and this enables your toddler to develop problem-solving skills.

As a parent, you may be tempted to minimize negative emotions observed in your kids. Why not tell them these feelings are normal. "You don't want to create a dynamic that only happiness is good.

Model Managing difficult feelings

For younger kids, teach them how you manage our own emotions so they model after you. At first, this might seem daunting, but it quickly clears away as they realize they are not alone anymore.

Some children who feel like big emotions sneak up on them can be helped with practice in recognizing their feelings,

The anger thermometer comes in handy here. Try ranking the intensity of your feelings from 1-10, with 1 being pretty calm and 10 being furious.

For example, if you forget something that you're meant to bring to Grandma's, quickly acknowledge that you are feeling frustrated and say that you're at a 4. It looks a little silly at first, but it teaches children to pause and notice what they are feeling at any given time.

If you see them starting to get upset about something, ask them what they are feeling, and how angry they are. Are they at a 6? For some younger kids, a visual aid like the feeling thermometer might help.

Communicate and Accept Your Child's Feelings

This is a process known as **Validation. It** is a powerful tool for helping kids calm down by

Taking them for whom they are and not always what we want .when a child feels understood, it has a profound effect on the child.

Sufficient validation means giving the needed attention to your kid. Follow them up, so you notice their body language and facial expressions and really understand their perspective. It gives you room to reflect if you are getting it right or missing it.

Helping kids by showing them that you're listening and trying to understand their experience can help avoid explosive behavior when a child is building towards a tantrum.

Try Active Ignoring

You do not always have to give attention to bad behavior. Sometimes Ignoring such practices like whining, arguing, inappropriate words or outbursts are a way to curb the repetition of negative emotion. You need to do this on purpose.

When turning away or leaving the room, you should be doing something else. After some time, if the kid is doing something right, then appreciate it and return your attention.

Give Positive Attention Always

This s a great way to get them to realize what you have been teaching. Children love attention and

When you're shaping a new behavior, you want to praise it and give a lot of attention to it. You need to be sincere here.

Covey Rules You Expect From Everyone

This is another way of keeping kids from expressing angry emotions. Do this when everyone is calm. When there is a Dependable structure, children feel they are in control.

Give advance warning so they will prepare accurately. Let them know what will happen after a particular thing they are already involved in. This will make them feel more in control and stay calmer

Provide and Give Options

If you need the cooperation of your children in doing something they are not enthusiastic about, giving them more than one option is probably the best way to go about it. This will reduce outbursts and increase compliance. For example: "John, please come with me to food shopping, or will you go with your Dad to pick up your sister."

Another example is Or: "please get ready for bed now, and we will read a story together — or you can get ready for bed in 15 minutes and no story."

This will reduce having to negotiate choices and leads to calmness.

Planning In Advance

You can talk about anything that may be challenging for your toddler in advance. Do this whenever there is relative calm so you get him or her prepared towards it. Also, discuss the possible negative emotional stress that may come later and how to manage it

For example, if you both visited her uncle and there was something that got her upset because she wasn't allowed to do it, whenever you return home, sit down and talk about it, so she will know what's allowed at uncle peters place.

Talking about stressful situations in advance helps avoid meltdowns. So by planning how things may turn out, we curtail many unnecessary emotional outbursts.

Revisit Previous Events

Whenever you revisit a prior occasion so everyone will learn from what happened the other day. It's not uncommon for parents to put past events away and hope for the best.

If a child has a tantrum, parents are often hesitant to bring it up later; on the other hand, we should bring it up in a nonjudgmental way.

This promotes critical thinking as kids start thinking about it and how to have a different outcome. This helps your child might remember them next time he's starting to feel overwhelmed.

Give Them 5 Individual Minutes Every Day

You have an essential role in helping your children manage stress and anger. Set five minutes a day to do something chosen by your child. This helps the child manage stress at other points in the day. It breeds a positive connection, without parental commands, this attention ignores any behavior but helps them be in charge.

If you have a kid who's having a tough time in school, he or she would be happy looking forward to that particular time. Always reinforce that 'I love you no matter what.

Calming Anger with the following Activities

1. **Breathe in and out.**

   Let the kids practice breathing to ease stress and regain confidence.

   Now breathe in, hold it a little, and breathe out. Repeat the steps

2. **I can count to five**

   Let the kids count from numbers one to five or one to ten

   1 2 3 4 5 6 7 8 9 10

3. **I can blow into my hands**

   Now take a moment and blow into your hands. Release the hands and blow again

4. **I can make a fist and relax my hand**

5. **I can do a body scan starting from my head**

   Starting from your head, now do all other parts too.

6. **I can ask for a hug**

Can I have a hug, please?

Sure, my dear.

7. I can sing a song

8. Play away your Anger

9. Read a storybook

10. WRITE A NOTE, NUMBERS OR ANYTHING USEFUL

11.DRAW A SCRIBBLE:

12. Paint and color

ANGER TRIGGERS

Do you use cutting words when you are angry

Yes _____ No _____

Do you look at others with an angry face?

Yes _____ No _____

Do you hit or kick someone?

Yes _____ No _____

Do you throw your toys and other things away?

Yes _____ No _____

Do you think it's ok to make fun of others

Yes _____ No _____

Anger triggers - what makes you angry

now list and mention some of the thins that make you angry

_____

_____

_____

_____

_____

_____

_____

every one of the things that you have listed above is common to many others. Everyone has them

remember its ok to feel angry

ANGER AFFECTS OTHERS

Do you know that anger affects others' STOP and THINK? Think about the other person's feelings and the consequences of inappropriately expressing your anger. It's like a boomerang bird. When it flies, it comes back to its starting point.

Every one of your angry feelings affects people- just like that bird comes back.

Try This

List some of the things you have experienced after expressing your anger among your friends.

1.

2.

3.

4.

5.

Always ask for help to calm down

The Anger thermometer

Now let's try to identify our feelings and know-how angry we are.

The Anger Thermometer:

Looking at the thermometer, see the colors and kindly answer these questions

LET'S TALK ABOUT EACH SECTION

What do you do when you are angry.?

Do you stomp your feet?

Yes [ ] No [ ]

Do you sigh loudly? Yes [ ] No [ ]

Do you growl? Yes [ ] No [ ]

Does your voice get louder? Yes [ ] No [ ]

Do you start invading other people's space?

Yes [ ] No [ ]

When some kids get angry, they yell?

Yes [ ] No [ ]

When some kids get angry, they are throwing things?

Yes [ ] No [ ]

When some kids get angry, do they running away?

Yes [ ] No [ ]

"When some kids get angry, they yell, is that something you do?"

Yes [ ] No [ ]

Furious

1. _____
   _____
2. _____
   _____

Angry

1. _____
   _____
2. _____
   _____

TOP – RED , BOTTOM - CALM

Tell me about a time you were at a red on the anger thermometer."

_____
_____
_____

Frustrated
1. _____
_____
2. _____
_____

Calm
1. _____
_____
2. _____
_____

_____

_____

"When you're at a yellow on the anger thermometer, what sort of things are you thinking about?"

_____

_____

_____

_____

_____

"How do you feel when you are at a green on the anger thermometer compared to a pink?"

_____

_____

_____

_____

_____

"If a stranger saw you when you were at green on the anger thermometer, how would they describe you?"

_____

_____

_____

_____

_____

_____

_____

_____

Anger Coloring Activities

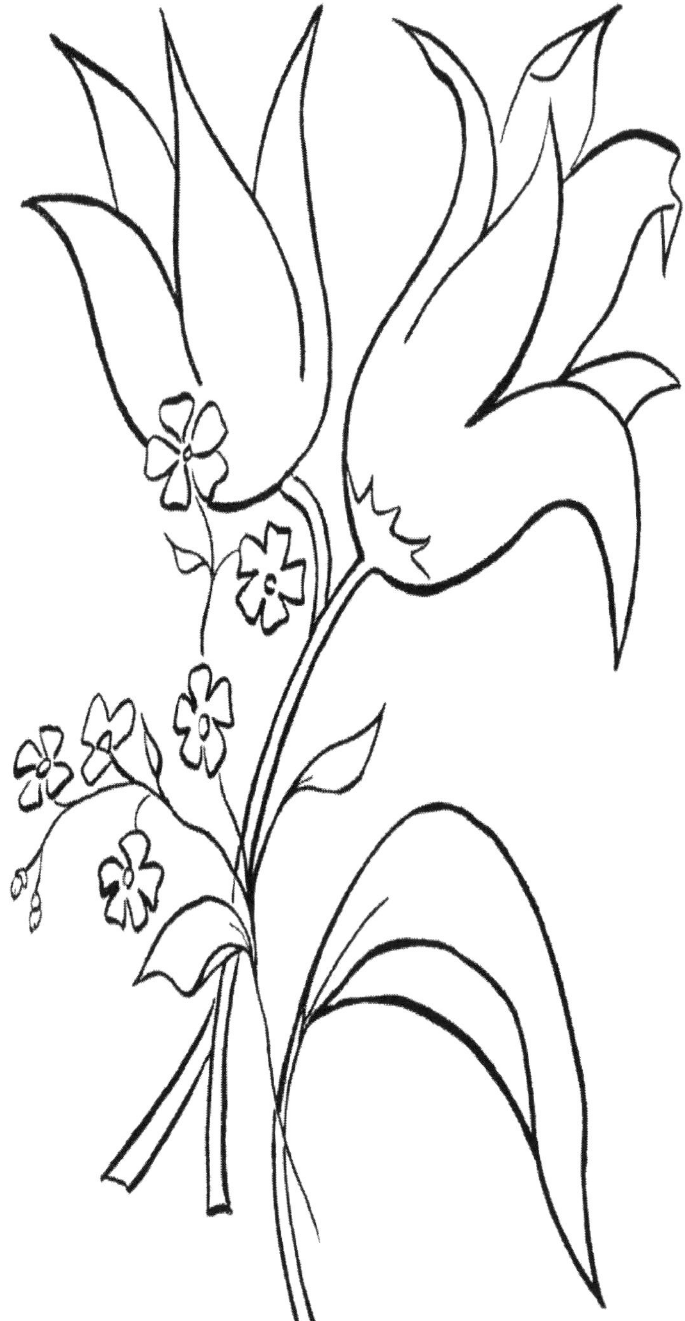

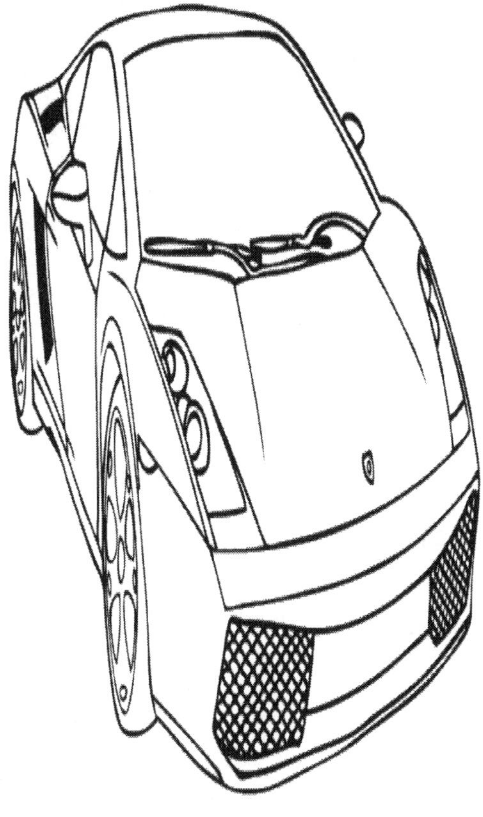

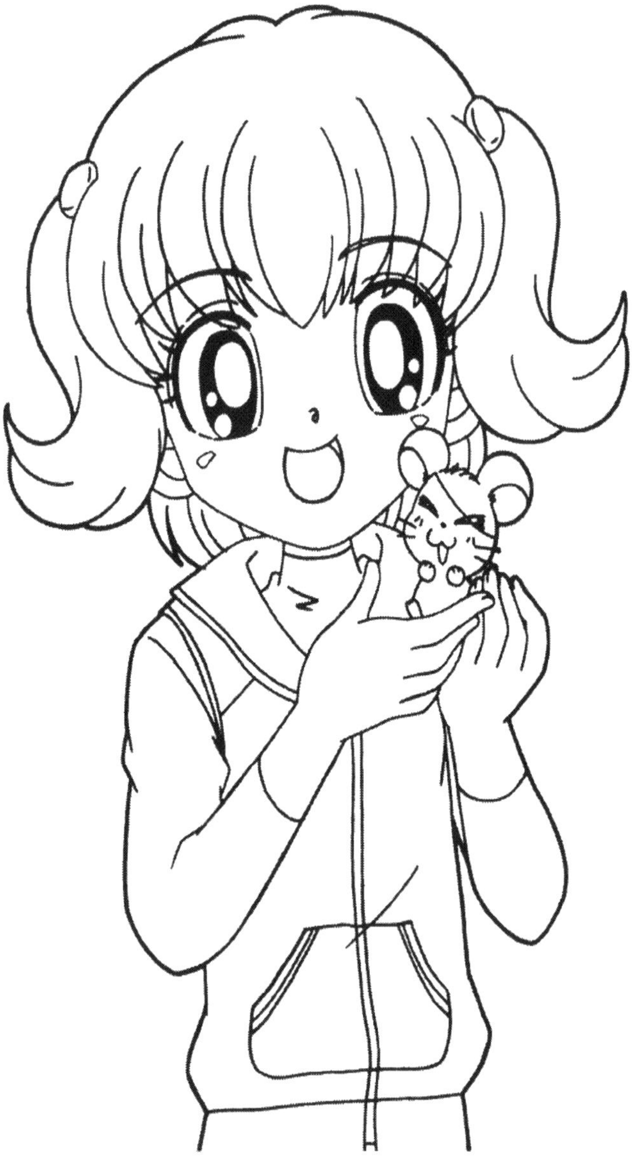

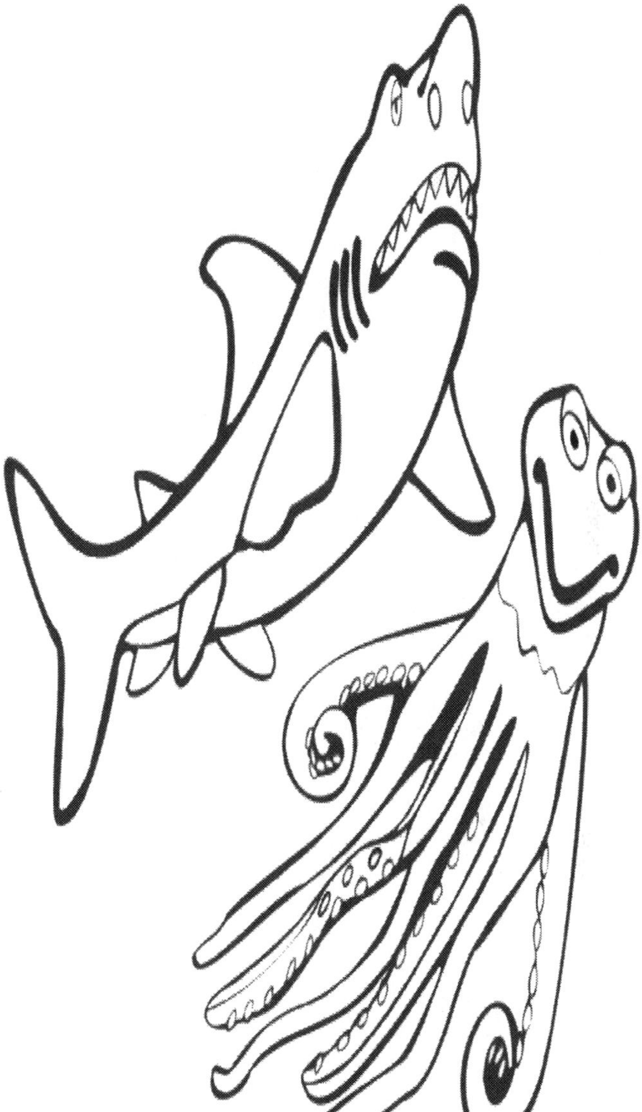

Help Kids do these Activities and Beat the Anger Daily

THE END

ABOUT THE AUTHOR

Samantha Williams is a mother of four kids, and she has been handling kids for a very long time. With her experience as a teacher, she takes her kids through each activity and lesson.

You can contact her through this email address.

seeminglygood@gmail.com

Kindly Leave a Review

Made in the USA
Columbia, SC
08 May 2020